21 DAYS TO A BETTER WOMAN!

"Prayer Challenge And Guide"

India T. Miller

Table Of Contents

Welcome to 21 Days To A Better Woman (with Bonus days) Prayer Challenge

It's a privilege bought at a tremendous price. Because of Jesus Christ and His sacrifice, all who follow Him become endowed with the Holy Spirit. And it is the Holy Spirit that enables our ability to communicate to, and be with, God. Before Christ, the followers of God could not communicate directly with Him, not in the way that we can today. That's why God established prophets and leaders to be a mouthpiece for Him on this Earth. But the people could not have a personal relationship with Him, until Christ died, resurrected and ascended to Heaven.

In Acts 2, we find the outpouring of the Holy Spirit and the beginning of a new era for humanity. In this new era, we get to have a relationship with God right here on Earth. As with any relationship, communication is key. Even though God knows everything, He still offers us the ability to speak with Him, a way for us to lean on and be guided directly by Him. God created humanity for fellowship and to have a relationship with Him, but that was all destroyed in the Garden when humanity ate from the forbidden tree. Through Christ's life and sacrifice, we are now able to be connected to God, and one way we do that is through prayer.

I thought this would be a good Challenge to help you turn to God in prayer over the next 21 days and beyond. I have provided you the tools you need for this Challenge.

In this Challenge, you'll find: An Entrance Worksheet: The questions in this worksheet will help you process how you presently think about quiet time and your relationship with God.

The 21 Day Challenge: Each day, you'll be provided with a Prayer Focal Point.

Simply put, this is a subject to direct your prayer attention. I include a little explanation of each Prayer Focal Point to help you better turn to God with the subject matter.

An Exit Worksheet: After completing the worksheet, you'll be asked to complete a final worksheet to process the Challenge, and to give you some ideas for moving forward with continuing your quiet time.

If you follow this Challenge, I believe you'll come out the other side with a profoundly new appreciation of God and the wonderful and good desires He has for your relationship with Him. Can you imagine how your life might look differently if you were able to see God's presence with you in all circumstances? That's my hope for you in taking this Challenge!

Entrance Worksheet

#1 Why are you taking this Challenge?

#2 What do you hope to get out of this

Challenge?

#3 What would you like to be different in your understanding and practice of prayer?

#4 What do you envision the fruit of prayer with God would look like for you?

#5 How do you see the God's presence in your life currently?

21 Days To A Better Woman Daily Guide

Day 1 Prayer Focal Point: Your Relationship With God

Guiding Thought: As with everything, it all boils down to you and God. Starting this Challenge off, we would like you to turn to God and speak with Him about your relationship. Ask Him for direction and guidance in growing closer to Him.

Notes:

_____

_____

_____

_____

_____

_____

_____

_____

_____

_____

_____

_____

_____

Day 2 Prayer Focal Point: Your Family

Guiding Thought: Lift up the members of your family to God today. Ask God where He is leading your family and how you can follow His call. Ask God where healing may be needed in your family and celebrate the joy your family has brought you.

Notes:

Day 3 Prayer Focal Point: Your Work

Guiding Thought: Even if you do not have "work," we all have tasks we do whether we are paid for or it or not. Reflect on the work you do throughout your day. Ask God to bring more of His purpose and will to your work.

Notes:

_____

_____

_____

_____

_____

_____

_____

_____

_____

_____

_____

_____

_____

_____

_____

_____

_____

_____

_____

Day 4 Prayer Focal Point: Your Friends

Guiding Thought: Reflect on your friends, both past and present. Lift up each name and ask God to show His love and grace on that person today. Also, thank God for these people and all of the joy and blessing they have brought to your life.

Notes:

Day 5 Prayer Focal Point: The Church

Guiding Thought: Pray for the the larger Church. The Church is always under attack from the enemy. Pray that God's will be done and seen through His Church.

Notes:

_____

_____

_____

_____

_____

_____

_____

_____

_____

_____

_____

_____

_____

_____

_____

_____

Day 6 Prayer Focal Point: People Who Are Suffering

Guiding Thought: People all around us are suffering, often silently. Lift up those who may be going through trials and ask God to give them peace and perseverance.

Notes:

_____

_____

_____

_____

_____

_____

_____

_____

_____

_____

_____

_____

_____

_____

_____

_____

_____

Day 7 Prayer Focal Point: Mentors In Your Life

Guiding Thought: Reflect on all the people who have shaped you into the person you are today. Thank God for those people, both past and present in your life.

Notes:

_____

_____

_____

_____

_____

_____

_____

_____

_____

_____

_____

_____

_____

_____

_____

_____

_____

Day 8 Prayer Focal Point: The World

Guiding Thought: The world is in desperate need of Jesus' love. Pray today for the world at large and for the realization of Christ among all people, all nations.

Notes:

_____

_____

_____

_____

_____

_____

_____

_____

_____

_____

_____

_____

_____

_____

_____

_____

_____

Day 9 Prayer Focal Point: Your Health

Guiding Thought: Health is something we all need, whether we have physical problems or not. The world we live in is very hostile and affects not only our bodies, but our hearts and minds as well. Spend some time reflecting on where you need God's healing in your life. Perhaps it is a physical healing or maybe an emotional one.

Notes:

_____

_____

_____

_____

_____

_____

_____

_____

_____

_____

_____

_____

_____

_____

_____

Day 10 Prayer Focal Point: Your Dreams, Ambition.

Guiding Thought: We all have, or had, dreams in our lives. Often times, dreams are not realized, for many reasons. What might you be dreaming of today? Bring it before God and ask Him to help you in your quest. Ask Him to reveal His will in your dream. Maybe you find yourself today without any dreams, talk to God about this and seek His will.

Notes:

Day 11 Prayer Focal Point: Government

Guiding Thought: Pray today for your local and national government. Pray that God's will be done and that the leaders would hear God in their lives and respond courageously to His call.

Notes:

_____

_____

_____

_____

_____

_____

_____

_____

_____

_____

_____

_____

_____

_____

_____

_____

_____

Day 12 Prayer Focal Point: Forgiveness

Guiding Thought: Jesus told the disciples that we should forgive not 7 times, but 7 times 70 (Matthew 18:22). Forgiveness is not natural to any of us; we all need God's power, grace and love to fully take our forgiveness to a new, holy level. Turn to God and ask Him to help you with those you may be harboring a grudge or past hurt. Ask God to help you release that pain into His arms. Ask Him for guidance on how to move forward.

Notes:

_____

_____

_____

_____

_____

_____

_____

_____

_____

_____

_____

_____

_____

_____

Day 13 Prayer Focal Point: Soldiers

Guiding Thought: Pray today for soldiers. Ask God to help them both on the field and when the return home. Many soldiers struggle with returning home after combat. Pray that God helps them transition back into their home life and seek the support they need.

Notes:

_____

_____

_____

_____

_____

_____

_____

_____

_____

_____

_____

_____

_____

_____

Day 14 Prayer Focal Point: People Affected By Natural Disaster

Guiding Thought: People all around the world are constantly faced with natural disaster. Tornadoes, hurricanes, floods, blizzards, earthquakes and other disasters can strike at any time. Lift up those who have recently, or currently, are facing natural disaster and ask God to bring them comfort, peace and His stability into their lives. Ask God to help them also receive the resources they need for survival.

Notes:

_____

_____

_____

_____

_____

_____

_____

_____

_____

_____

_____

_____

_____

_____

Day 15 Prayer Focal Point: People Who Do Not Know Or Follow God

Guiding Thought: There are many people in our world and in our personal lives who do not know Jesus. Pray specifically for those people today and ask the Lord to come into their lives.

Notes:

_____

_____

_____

_____

_____

_____

_____

_____

_____

_____

_____

_____

_____

_____

_____

_____

_____

_____

Day 16 Prayer Focal Point: People You Have Hurt

Guiding Thought: Unfortunately, there are people in your life you have hurt. It is part of being human; we are not perfect. Whether you intended it or not, people have been hurt by your actions, or inactions. Ask God to reveal someone you have unintentionally hurt and seek His guidance on what He would like you to do. Or perhaps you already know of the person or people you have hurt. In that case, turn to God and speak to Him about the situation and ask for His direction on how to proceed.

Notes:

Day 17 Prayer Focal Point: Christian Leaders

Guiding Thought: Christian leaders always need prayer. Since we live in a world operated by darkness, Christian leaders are always under attack. Pray that God's presence always outshines darkness in their lives. Pray that they do not fall under temptation to follow the ways of the world and that God is their primary pursuit.

Notes:

Day 18 Prayer Focal Point: Your Neighbors

Guiding Thought: We all have neighbors. Maybe you know them, maybe you don't. Regardless, pray for them today. Ask that God's presence is realized among them today and that there day is filled with His goodness. This is how you can bless them today.

Notes:

Day 19 Prayer Focal Point: Your Stress

Guiding Thought: What is it that is stressing you today? Maybe it's bills? Health issues? Children? Family or work problems? Personal pursuits? Whatever it is that is occupying your heart and mind, turn to God with the stressor in hand and give it over to Him today. Ask for help in trusting that He is good and will honor your request. Repeat this practice as much as needed, because stress is not easily defeated with one mere prayer.

Notes:

Day 20 Prayer Focal Point: Your Calling

Guiding Thought: Do you realize we all have a calling? Most are not called to professional Christian work, but we are all called to work in the Kingdom of Heaven. Maybe you already are aware of your calling. If so, turn to God and continue to seek His guidance and Fruit in your calling. If you are not sure what you are called to do, turn to God and start a dialogue about where He is calling you and equipping you to serve.

Notes:

_____

_____

_____

_____

_____

_____

_____

_____

_____

_____

_____

_____

_____

_____

Day 21 Prayer Focal Point: Children

Guiding Thought: Children are the most innocent in our world and need the most guidance. Whether you have children or not, bring before the Lord the children you know in your life and pray for His protection, guidance and love over their lives.

Notes:

Bonus Days

Day 22 Prayer Focal Point: Enemies

Guiding Thought: Pray today for your enemies. Try to think of all of the people who are your enemies. Maybe it is people in your everyday life, or perhaps you consider your enemies to be political leaders or other notable figures. Turn to God with all the people who you find fault with and talk to Him about why they bother you. Seek God's guidance and will as you speak with Him about your enemies.

Notes:

_____

_____

_____

_____

_____

_____

_____

_____

_____

_____

_____

_____

Day 23 Prayer Focal Point: Your Christian Community

Guiding Thought: Pray today for your Christian community, your local church, your fellow Christian companions. Ask God for His protection, guidance and love in their lives.

Notes:

Day 24 Prayer Focal Point: Your Worries

Guiding Thought: What is of concern to you today? What are you worried about? Bring your concern(s) before God and know that He will guide you through your worries. Ask Him for His wisdom in this matter and trust that He will provide the answer.

Notes:

Day 25 Prayer Focal Point: Your Joys

Guiding Thought: What is it that brings you joy? Maybe it's certain people, activities, work, nature and so on. Reflect on all those things and thank God for these wonderful gifts in your life.

Notes:

Day 26 Prayer Focal Point: Where You Live

Guiding Thought: Thank God for where you reside. Thank Him for how He has provided a shelter over your head and food in your belly.

Notes:

_____

_____

_____

_____

_____

_____

_____

_____

_____

_____

_____

_____

_____

_____

_____

_____

_____

Day 27 Prayer Focal Point: Disadvantaged Nations

Guiding Thought: There are many countries in dyer need of the basics of life, like clean water, substantial food and safety. Pray for all those nations today, and that God's provision would be found among them. Ask God if there is any way you could help this epidemic. Day

Notes:

Day 28 Prayer Focal Point: Rest

Guiding Thought: Thank God today for the ability to rest. Speak to Him about how you use this necessary gift. Seek His will in your utilization of rest and listen for His direction. Day

Notes:

_____

_____

_____

_____

_____

_____

_____

_____

_____

_____

_____

_____

_____

_____

_____

_____

_____

Day 29 Prayer Focal Point: Your Salvation

Guiding Thought: Spend time thinking about your life before following Christ. Thank God for all the wonderfulness He has brought you in your life because you chose to follow Him. Reflect, with God, on what life will look like in perfection, which is Heaven.

Notes:

_____

_____

_____

_____

_____

_____

_____

_____

_____

_____

_____

_____

_____

_____

_____

_____

_____

_____

Day 30 - Final Reflection Prayer Focal Point: Love

Guiding Thought: What would your world look like if it didn't have any love in it? Turn to God and thank Him for showing you what love is and blessing you with His love in your life. Try to imagine the world if God's love was not in it at all. Ask God how you might realize His Fruit of love more in your life and show it better to those you interact with throughout your days.

Thank You I hope this challenge was an amazing one, where you did grow closer to God. It is through devotion and discipline that we draw closer to God. To be a disciple means to be disciplined, and that is just what you accomplished this month. It is my hope that you carry forth from this Challenge and continuing turning to God through prayer. Prayer truly is a privilege that we get because of Jesus Christ's sacrifice. I hope that you have grown in your communication with God this month.

Notes:

Exit Worksheet

#1. Now that you've finished this Challenge, what were the past 30 days like for you?

#2. How might you incorporate more prayer into your daily routine?

#3. Did you notice anything change during your day, by intentionally praying everyday, example: find yourself reacting differently; more aware of God's presence with you all day, and so forth?

#4. What are some of the ways that you have seen God's presence manifest in your own life?

#5. What are areas where you need to recognize more of God's presence in your life?

#6. Are there images in your mind that help you better visualize the powerful nature of God's presence?

#7. Carrying forth from this Challenge, how might you continue praying everyday? What could you establish in your routine to help you turn to God and grow in your relationship with Him?

21 Spiritual Action Steps for Women

1. **Start Each Day with Prayer**

   Begin your morning by inviting God into your day, asking for guidance and strength.

2. **Read a Daily Scripture**

   Commit to reading a Bible verse or passage daily to renew your mind.

3. **Keep a Prayer Journal**

   Write down your prayers, God's answers, and reflections on His Word.

4. **Practice Gratitude**

   List 3 things you're thankful for each day to cultivate a joyful heart.

5. **Fast Regularly**

   Choose a day or meal to fast, seeking deeper clarity and spiritual breakthrough.

6. **Memorize Key Verses**

   Hide God's Word in your heart to recall in times of challenge.

7. **Attend or host a Women's Bible Study**

   Connect with other women for encouragement, learning, and accountability.

8. **Serve Others**

Volunteer your time or talents to bless someone in need.

9. **Spend Time in Worship**

Sing or listen to worship music that uplifts your spirit and draws you closer to God.

10. **Practice Forgiveness**

Release bitterness and forgive those who have hurt you.

11. **Meditate on God's Promises**

Reflect deeply on the promises God has made in Scripture.

12. **Speak Life**

Use your words to encourage, bless, and build up others.

13. **Set Boundaries**

Protect your time and energy to focus on spiritual growth.

14. **Practice Silence and Solitude**

Regularly take quiet time to listen for God's voice.

15. **Seek Spiritual Mentorship**

Find a mature believer to guide and challenge your faith journey.

16. **Confess and Repent Regularly**

Keep your heart clean before God by acknowledging sin.

17. **Pray for Others**

Intercede for family, friends, leaders, and those in need.

18. **Journal God's Faithfulness**

   Write down how God has worked in your life to boost your faith.

19. **Live with Integrity**

   Align your actions with your beliefs, even when no one is watching.

20. **Celebrate Small Victories**

   Recognize and thank God for every step forward in your spiritual walk.

21. **Share Your Testimony**

   Tell others what God has done in your life to encourage their faith.

Who Am I!!!!!!!!!

I am your constant companion.

I am your greatest helper or your heaviest burden.

I will push you onward or drag you down to failure.

I am completely at your command.

Half the things you do, you might just as well turn over to me, and I will be able to do them quickly and correctly.

I am easily managed; you must merely be firm with me. Show me exactly how you want something done, and after a few lessons I will do it automatically.

I am the servant of all great men.

And, alas, of all failures as well.

Those who are great, I have made great. Those who are failures, I have made failures.

I am not a machine, though I work with all the precision of a machine.

Plus, the intelligence of a man.

You may run me for profit, or run me for ruin; it makes no difference to me.

Take me, train me, be firm with me and I will put the world at your feet.

Be easy with me, and I will destroy you.

Who am I?

I am a HABIT!

Spiritual Growth Plan

Step 1: Renew Your Commitment to Christ

- **Daily Surrender Prayer** – Start each day by surrendering your plans, thoughts, and heart to Jesus.

    o *Example: "Lord, I give this day to You. Lead me, teach me, and draw me closer to You."*

- **Ask for Spiritual Renewal** – Pray for God to ignite a deeper hunger for Him.

    o *Psalm 51:10 – "Create in me a pure heart, O God, and renew a steadfast spirit within me."*

Step 2: Deepen Your Relationship with God

Bible Study Plan

- Read the Bible with intentionality.
- Choose a structured reading plan (e.g., Gospel of John, Psalms, or a Bible-in-a-year plan).
- **Reflect & Apply:** After reading, ask:

    1. What does this teach me about God?
    2. How can I apply this today?

James 1:22 – "Do not merely listen to the word… Do what it says."

Develop a Passionate Prayer Life

- Pray beyond requests—spend time worshiping, listening, and confessing.

- Keep a prayer journal to track prayers and answered prayers.

- Set reminders for "mini-prayers" throughout the day (e.g., thanking God, asking for wisdom).

📖 *1 Thessalonians 5:16-18 – "Rejoice always, pray continually, give thanks in all circumstances."*

Step 3: Step Out in Faith

Serve & Love Others

- Find ways to serve in your church or community.

- Ask God to open your eyes to someone in need each day.

- Look for opportunities to encourage, give, or help others.

📖 *Mark 10:45 – "For even the Son of Man did not come to be served, but to serve."*

Share Your Faith Boldly

- Pray for opportunities to share Christ with others.

- If you're hesitant, start by sharing how God is working in your life.

- Be willing to stand for biblical truth, even when it's uncomfortable.

📖 *Matthew 5:16 – "Let your light shine before others, that they may see your good deeds and glorify your Father in heaven."*

Step 4: Cultivate a Spirit-Filled Life

Surround Yourself with Godly Influences

- Join a Bible study or discipleship group.

- Listen to sermons, Christian podcasts, or worship music regularly.

- Choose friendships that encourage spiritual growth.

Proverbs 27:17 – "As iron sharpens iron, so one person sharpens another."

Fast & Remove Spiritual Distractions

- Identify things that pull you away from God (excessive TV, social media, busyness).

- Consider fasting (from food, entertainment, or distractions) to focus on God.

- Spend quiet time alone with God to hear His voice.

Psalm 46:10 – "Be still, and know that I am God."

Step 5: Keep Growing & Stay Accountable

Set Growth Goals

- Example Goals:

- ☑ Read the Bible daily for 30 days.

- ☑ Pray intentionally for 10 minutes every morning.

- ☑ Memorize one Bible verse per week.

Find an Accountability Partner

- Ask a friend, mentor, or church leader to check in with you on your spiritual walk.

- Be honest about struggles and victories.

Ecclesiastes 4:9-10 – "Two are better than one... If either of them falls down, one can help the other up."

Final Encouragement

Growth takes time! Don't get discouraged if you struggle. God is patient and loves when we take steps toward Him. Keep seeking, keep trusting, and keep growing!

Philippians 1:6 – "He who began a good work in you will carry it on to completion until the day of Christ Jesus."

Let's Continue, "30 more Bonus Days."

30-Day Prayer Focal Points for Women:

Your Relationship with God

Day 1: Draw Near to God

Scripture: James 4:8

Prayer Focus: Invite God to draw close; seek Him with all your heart.

Action: Spend 15-30 minutes in quiet prayer and journaling about your desire for intimacy with God.

Day 2: Know God's Love

Scripture: Romans 8:38-39

Prayer Focus: Meditate on God's unconditional, unchanging love.

Action: Write down ways God has shown His love in your life.

Day 3: Trust God's Plan

Scripture: Proverbs 3:5-6

Prayer Focus: Surrender your plans and fears to God's perfect guidance.

Action: Journal your worries and surrender them in prayer.

Day 4: Hear God's Voice

Scripture: John 10:27

Prayer Focus: Ask God to help you recognize His voice daily.

Action: Spend time listening quietly and note any impressions or Scriptures that come to mind.

Day 5: Walk in Faith

Scripture: 2 Corinthians 5:7

Prayer Focus: Pray for courage to trust God even when you can't see the whole path.

Action: Identify one area where God is calling you to step out in faith.

Day 6: Embrace God's Grace

Scripture: Ephesians 2:8-9

Prayer Focus: Thank God for His unearned grace and mercy.

Action: Reflect on moments you've experienced grace and jot them down.

Day 7: Be Still Before God

Scripture: Psalm 46:10

Prayer Focus: Practice stillness and quiet your soul before the Lord.

Action: Take a 10-minute silent pause during your day and focus solely on God's presence.

Day 8: Renew Your Mind

Scripture: Romans 12:2

Prayer Focus: Ask God to transform your thoughts and attitudes.

Action: Identify any negative thoughts to surrender and replace with God's truth.

Day 9: Delight in God's Word

Scripture: Psalm 1:2-3

Prayer Focus: Ask God to make His Word your daily delight and guide.

Action: Commit to reading a Psalm or Proverbs each day this week.

Day 10: Celebrate God's Faithfulness

Scripture: Lamentations 3:22-23

Prayer Focus: Praise God for His consistent faithfulness in your life.

Action: List testimonies of God's faithfulness you have experienced.

Day 11: Rest in God's Presence

Scripture: Matthew 11:28-30

Prayer Focus: Bring your burdens to Jesus and rest in Him.

Action: Practice deep breathing and releasing stress to God during prayer.

Day 12: Ask for Wisdom

Scripture: James 1:5

Prayer Focus: Pray for God's wisdom in your daily decisions.

Action: Write down a situation where you need divine insight.

Day 13: Live Out God's Love

Scripture: 1 John 4:7-8

Prayer Focus: Ask God to help you love others as He loves you.

Action: Perform an act of kindness or encouragement today.

Day 14: Seek God's Peace

Scripture: Philippians 4:6-7

Prayer Focus: Invite God's peace to calm any anxiety or fear

Action: Practice prayerful surrender of worries as they arise.

Day 15: Grow in Humility

Scripture: Micah 6:8

Prayer Focus: Ask God to cultivate humility and kindness in your heart.

Action: Reflect on ways to serve others with a humble heart.

Day 16: Confess and Receive Forgiveness

Scripture: 1 John 1:9

Prayer Focus: Bring your shortcomings to God and accept His forgiveness.

Action: Write a prayer of confession and gratitude for God's mercy.

Day 17: Walk in Obedience

Scripture: John 14:15

Prayer Focus: Commit to obeying God's voice and promptings.

Action: Identify one area God is calling you to obey today.

Day 18: Strengthen Your Prayer Life

Scripture: 1 Thessalonians 5:17

Prayer Focus: Ask God to help you pray continually and with faith.

Action: Set a reminder to pray through your day's schedule.

Day 19: Cultivate Gratitude

Scripture: 1 Thessalonians 5:18

Prayer Focus: Thank God for all circumstances, big and small.

Action: Keep a gratitude journal for the next week.

Day 20: Trust God in Waiting

Scripture: Psalm 27:14

Prayer Focus: Pray for patience and hope during seasons of waiting.

Action: Reflect on a past time God showed up after a wait.

Day 21: Seek God's Kingdom First

Scripture: Matthew 6:33

Prayer Focus: Commit to prioritizing God's kingdom and righteousness.

Action: Evaluate how you can put God first in your daily routines.

Day 22: Walk in Freedom

Scripture: Galatians 5:1

Prayer Focus: Pray for freedom from anything holding you captive.

Action: Identify and pray against any spiritual or emotional bondage.

Day 23: Be a Light to Others

Scripture: Matthew 5:14-16

Prayer Focus: Ask God to use you as a beacon of His love and truth.

Action: Share an encouraging word or testimony with someone.

Day 24: Embrace Your Identity in Christ

Scripture: 2 Corinthians 5:17

Prayer Focus: Meditate on who you are in Christ and your new identity.

Action: Write affirmations based on your identity in Him.

Day 25: Practice Forgiveness

Scripture: Colossians 3:13

Prayer Focus: Ask God to help you forgive those who have hurt you.

Action: Pray for anyone you struggle to forgive.

Day 26: Live with Joy

Scripture: Nehemiah 8:10

Prayer Focus: Pray to experience God's joy regardless of circumstances.

Action: Do something today that brings you joy and thank God for it.

Day 27: Seek Spiritual Growth

Scripture: 2 Peter 3:18

Prayer Focus: Ask God to help you grow in grace and knowledge.

Action: Choose a book, podcast, or study to deepen your faith.

Day 28: Serve with a Glad Heart

Scripture: Galatians 5:13

Prayer Focus: Pray for a willing and joyful heart in service.

Action: Volunteer or help someone in need today.

Day 29: Remain Hopeful

Scripture: Romans 15:13

Prayer Focus: Ask God to fill you with hope and peace through faith.

Action: Write a letter to your future self encouraging hope.

Day 30: Commit to Life-long Relationship(Discipleship)

Scripture: Revelation 3:20

Prayer Focus: Recommit your life to daily walking with God.

Action: Write a personal covenant or prayer of commitment.

More Resources

How to Start a Devotional

Starting a devotional

can feel like a daunting task. Have you ever wondered how to begin? How do you carve out time each day for spiritual reflection and growth? Whether you're new to devotionals or looking to establish a deeper connection, this guide is for you.

In this step-by-step journey, we'll explore how to start a devotional that's not only meaningful but also sustainable. With practical tips, scripture references, and helpful examples, you'll discover how to create a routine that draws you closer to God. Ready to dive in? Let's explore the transformative power of daily devotionals and how you can make them a central part of your life.

HOW TO START A DEVOTIONAL
A Step-by-Step Guide

#1. Understand the Purpose of a Devotional

Before beginning your devotional, it's crucial to first understand its deeper purpose. A devotional is not just a task to check off your list—it's an intentional, focused time designed to deepen your relationship with God. It's a chance to set aside distractions and give your attention to His word and presence. Devotionals help to center your thoughts on God and His promises, allowing you to reflect on His greatness and apply His wisdom in your life. The purpose of a devotional is spiritual growth, cultivating intimacy with God through regular encounters with His Word. By understanding this purpose, your approach to devotionals becomes more intentional, knowing that each time you sit down, it's an opportunity for transformation.

#2. Choose a Time and Place

Choosing a consistent time and place for your devotional is essential in cultivating a habit. You need to find a moment during your day when you can be fully present, undistracted, and intentional about connecting with God. Some people prefer early mornings, as it sets the tone for the rest of their day, while others might find evenings or quiet times during lunch break to be best. The key is consistency—make it a part of your routine, like brushing your teeth. You want your devotional time to be sacred, so finding a space where you won't be interrupted is just as important as choosing the right time. Create a quiet environment that fosters focus and reflection, whether it's a cozy chair, a window-side nook, or a peaceful corner of your home. If you're always on the go, even a moment in a park or a peaceful car ride can be a good spot to connect with God.

#3. Select Your Devotional Material

There's an abundance of devotional material to choose from, but it's important to select something that resonates with you and serves your current spiritual needs. You might start with a traditional Bible, a devotional book, or even a digital app. Many devotionals focus on a specific theme, such as hope, forgiveness, or gratitude, while others guide you through books of the Bible or daily Scripture reading plans. A great starting point is to look for a devotional that helps you build discipline in your spiritual life and connects you with Scripture. Consider what you need in this season of your life—whether it's deepening your Bible knowledge, cultivating gratitude, or strengthening your prayer life. If you are unsure, try using a simple Bible reading plan. You can also follow along with a daily devotional app or book that challenges you to reflect on Scripture every day. You don't need the fanciest or most complex materials to begin—just something that helps you draw closer to God each day.

#4. Follow a Simple Devotional Structure

A structured approach helps keep your devotional time focused and effective. While it's easy to feel overwhelmed by the idea of what to do or how to pray, sticking to a simple structure gives clarity to your time with God. Here's a simple devotional structure you can follow:

- **Prayer:** Begin with a short prayer, asking God to open your heart to what He wants to speak to you. Invite the Holy Spirit to guide your time.

- **Scripture:** Read a passage from the Bible, allowing yourself to reflect on what God is saying through His word. Don't rush through it—take your time and let the meaning settle in.

- **Application:** Think about how the Scripture applies to your life today. Is there an area where you need to grow, or a specific action God is calling you to take?

- **Prayer:** Conclude by praying through the insights you've gained. Ask God for the strength to apply His word in your life, and express gratitude for His presence.

This simple structure will keep you grounded and ensure that your time is focused, allowing you to go deeper in your reflection without feeling lost or overwhelmed.

#5. Keep It Simple and Consistent

Simplicity is powerful. Your devotional doesn't need to be long or complicated for it to be meaningful. The goal is to establish a habit, and the best way to do this is by keeping it simple. A 10-minute devotional might be just as impactful as a 30-minute session if it's done consistently. Instead of pressuring yourself to have long sessions, focus on showing up every day, even for a brief moment. You can read one verse, reflect for a few minutes, and pray. Over time, you'll see the benefits of this consistency, and the habit will become ingrained in your life. It's more important to build a habit of spending time with God regularly than to spend hours trying to cover every detail. Start small and build from there, remembering that even five minutes a day can create lasting spiritual growth.

#6. Be Flexible and Allow for Growth

While consistency is important, flexibility is key. Life has a way of throwing curveballs—there may be days when you miss your devotional time or when you need to adjust the length or structure. That's okay. Devotionals should be flexible enough to grow with you. If you find yourself getting distracted or feeling spiritually dry, it might be time to switch things up. Perhaps you're in a season where you need a different devotional material or a new time of day. If your schedule changes, allow your devotional practice to adapt. Embrace growth, knowing that there will be seasons where your devotionals look different. The beauty of flexibility is that it gives you room to explore and grow, so don't be discouraged by an imperfect routine. As long as you keep your heart open to God, He will meet you wherever you are.

#7. Apply What You Learn

A devotional is not just about learning—it's about applying what you've learned to your life. It's easy to read a verse or a passage and move on, but the real transformation happens when you let Scripture shape your actions, thoughts, and decisions. Take time to consider how the verse or the insight applies to your everyday life. Are there relationships that need mending? Are you struggling with anxiety or fear that God's word speaks to? How can you live out what you've read? Ask the Holy Spirit to help you apply the truths you've discovered in your devotional time. Don't just let it be an intellectual exercise—let it impact your emotions, actions, and relationships. This is where growth occurs. The more you apply Scripture, the more you'll experience its transformative power in your life.

#8. Seek Accountability and Community

While your devotional time is deeply personal, it doesn't have to be a solo endeavor. Engaging with others in your faith journey adds depth, accountability, and encouragement. Sharing what you're learning with a friend, a spouse, or a small group can help you stay committed and deepen your understanding. When you talk about what you've discovered, it reinforces the lessons and provides different perspectives. Find someone who can hold you accountable, check in with your devotional habits, and encourage you along the way. Community is also a powerful tool for spiritual growth. Being a part of a group that shares the same goal of growing closer to God can keep you motivated and inspired. Whether it's attending a Bible study, joining an online group, or having regular check-ins with a friend, being accountable to others is an invaluable part of your devotional life.

You Can Be Better In 21 Days

Completing this 21 day Challenge and Starting a devotional is a powerful step toward deepening your relationship with God and becoming a Better Woman By understanding purpose, creating a consistent routine, and applying what you learn, you'll experience spiritual growth and transformation. Remember, simplicity and consistency are key.

Be flexible, stay accountable, and allow your devotional time to evolve as you grow. Most importantly, keep your heart open to God's presence and guidance. Whether your devotionals last five minutes or thirty, the time you spend with God will always be worthwhile. Start today, and watch your faith flourish as you draw closer to Him each day. God Bless You on Your Journey.

Made in the USA
Columbia, SC
16 July 2025

60780696R10037